~IN MY~ DESERT

BY PAT MORA
ILLUSTRATED BY
SHONTO BEGAY

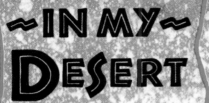

CELEBRATION PRESS
Pearson Learning Group

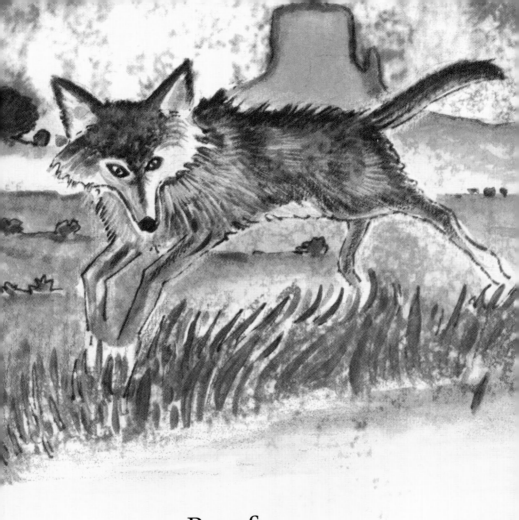

Run fox, run.

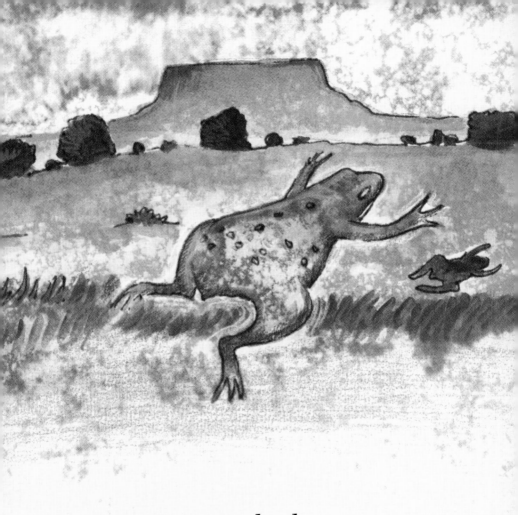

Hop toads, hop.

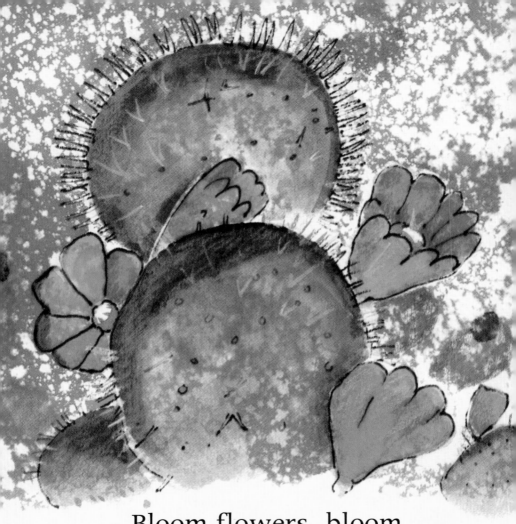

Bloom flowers, bloom.

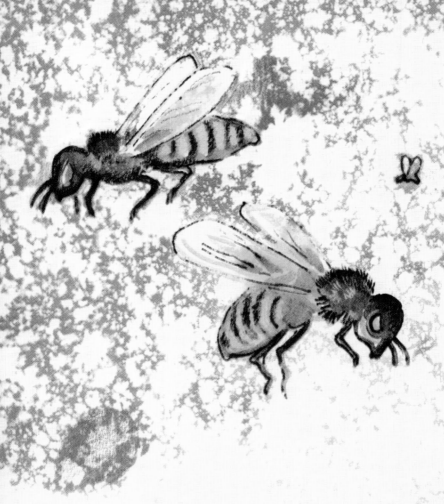

Zoom bees, zoom.

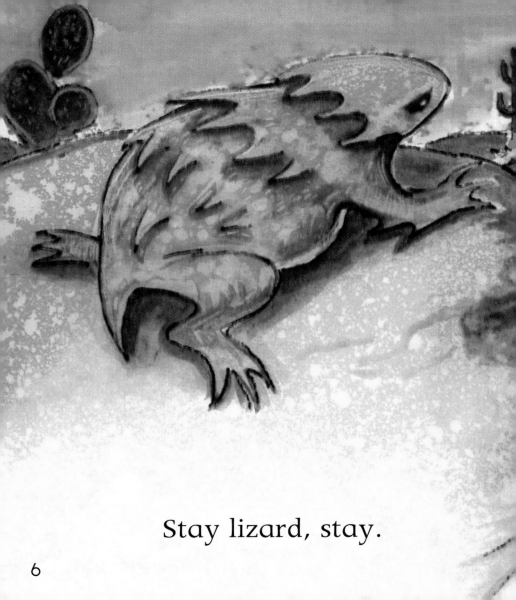

Stay lizard, stay.

6

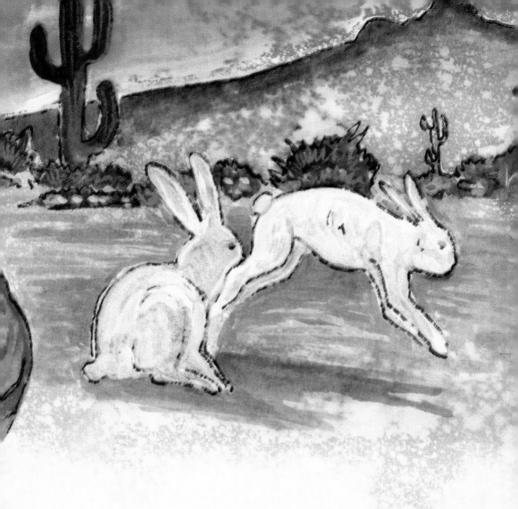

Play rabbits, play.

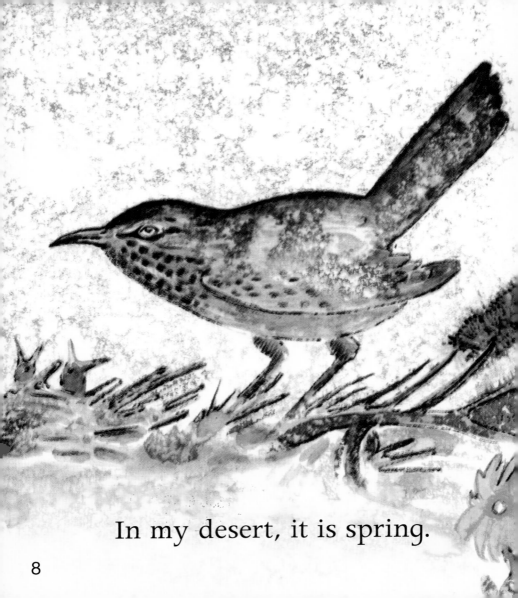

In my desert, it is spring.